C.H.A.R.A.C.T.E.R.

Nine Essentials to Excellent Customer Service and Increased Profitability

RENÉE L. BROWN

Printed in the United States of America

First Printing, 2019

978-0-578-60010-9

Godly Women's Network

Chattanooga, TN 37421

If you are interested in Renée as a keynote speaker, motivational speaker, panelist, or workshop presenter, contact her at:

Reneebrown1@yahoo.com
www.girlfriendsofvirtue.com
(248) 250-0159

Preface

I have come to realize that CHARACTER is the key to abundant living. Like many people, I spent most of my life trying to please other people and defining my value by what others thought of me. While oftentimes, the thoughts of others about me were great as long as I was performing according to their standards; the problem came when I fell short of what I thought determined my self-worth.

After graduating from law school, while America was reeling from the economic recession of 2007, I found myself feeling like a failure. After turning down a few offers and not getting the one offer I believed was for me, I was jobless and soon became homeless. This period became one of the most difficult seasons of my life. However, unbeknownst to me, it became the beginning of my personal transformation.

As a Christian and follower of Jesus Christ, I was taught to be God-like, but unfortunately, I was unaware of what exactly this entailed. When my world came tumbling down God used this time to give birth to the real Renée Brown. More than two years after completing law school and failing the Texas Bar Exam, a friend of mine came to me and said God led her to tell me to make an acronym out of the word girlfriends and write a book. What? I snapped back. Being obedient to the Holy Spirit I followed suit. Then the following words came to me: God-fearing, Intelligent, Resilient, Loving, Faithful, Reliable, Influential, Enthusiastic, Noble, Diligent and Spiritual. Then I was led to search the bible for an understanding of each word. As I did this, I discovered immediately who I was as one created in the image of God and who I was not based upon my lack of knowledge.

This would begin my journey to discover my true character, which would then manifest my authenticity and produce my transformation. As I grew, I realized how one's CHARACTER is the key to personal and professional success. I started to apply my experience and knowledge to every aspect of my life, and beginning in 2019 my metamorphosis was complete, and I was reborn.

My purpose has been revealed, and I am committed to teaching CHARACTER principles to people in all spaces and places. I am an enthusiastic speaker and engaging storyteller who works with businesses, educators, government leaders, and individuals seeking to transform themselves and their environments to become more customer service oriented and prosperous.

As an engaging storyteller, I teach and train others how to discover their true CHARACTER, live authentically and transform their lives to live more prosperous.

Introduction

C.H.A.R.A.C.T.E.R.

Nine Essentials to Excellent Customer Service and Increased Profitability

The greatest challenges for many small to mid-size businesses are increasing revenues and hiring and retaining quality employees.

Businesses may seek to increase revenues by obtaining more market share. However, without a commitment to customer attraction, retention, and satisfaction, desires to become more profitable will not be achieved. Furthermore, solely focusing on retaining a few particularly large clients, is not the strategy, nor in the best interest of the company.

The role of customer service has expanded over the past few decades. At one time, the discussion of this subject was relegated to the service industry and call centers. Today customer service is what distinguishes the good companies from the great. Any business that wants to be a leader understands that customer service is an integral part of the entire organization and is a prerequisite for success.

A business customer service philosophy must include relationships with all its publics and employees. This will govern not only the way it treats the customer who receives the goods and/or services; but the care of its employees that help produce those goods and/or services. A customer service focus is vital to the bottom line of any business. It guides the quality of relationships a business has with its customers, employees, and supplier partners. Customer service is fundamental to hiring quality employees and increasing profits because it reflects the heart and values of a company.

"C.H.A.R.A.C.T.E.R., Nine Essentials to Excellent Customer Service and Increased Profitability" will enlighten you on the key characteristics a business needs to attract quality employees and customers. It will encourage you to embody these traits so they are increasingly manifested by every employee and experienced by all customers. Your business will be inspired to make immediate adoption of these qualities and be positioned to positively affect profitability. Moreover, your business will develop character traits, which will result in Excellent Customer Service and Increased Profitability. As you practice the Nine Essentials, the desired outcomes of increasing revenues and hiring and retaining quality employees will materialize.

Key Character traits

Compassion, **Humility**, **Attentive**, **Resilient**, **Assertive**, **Conscientious**, **Thankful**, **Enthusiastic** and **Reliable**

C.H.A.R.A.C.T.E.R. and Soft-Skills Development Training

Training Objectives

To develop individuals and /or groups who will possess the character traits and soft skills necessary to effectively provide high-quality customer service.

Learning Objectives

At the end of this program, participants shall be able to do the following:

1. Explain key character traits and soft skills

2. Articulate how to utilize these traits and skills at work and in their personal life

3. Face any challenge or difficulty with courage and confidence

4. Handle unpleasant situations kindly and peacefully

5. Demonstrate their good character in the social and work environment by managing individual emotions

6. Creatively showcase one's character and soft skills

Definition of Character Traits and Soft Skills

Character is what you value. Values establish your beliefs, and your beliefs determine your desires and actions.
Renée L. Brown

Character traits produce soft skills that determine the way a person thinks and behaves with other people. These traits and skills are typically a definite part of one's personality, which dictates how one interacts with others. On the other hand, hard or technical skills have to do with the knowledge one possesses in a specific area. For instance, the technical skills required for a lawyer would include the ability to read and interpret laws, active listening, and attention to detail. Conversely, the soft skills essential for a lawyer are compassion, humility, resilience, and reliability.

This training program introduces participants to nine key character traits that are vital to overcoming challenges and obstacles faced in the workplace and in life and discusses the importance of these traits and skills with participants.

Character traits and soft skills are important because they help participants:

1. To develop and sustain interpersonal relationships

2. To make appropriate and reasonable decisions regardless of circumstances

3. To communicate with excellence and professionalism

4. To provide high-quality service and performance

Key Character traits

Compassion

Humility

Attentive

Resilient

Assertive

Conscientious

Thankful

Enthusiastic

Reliable

#1 - Compassion

*"Compassion is the keen awareness of the
interdependence of all things."*
Thomas Merton

Compassion is to have a sympathetic consciousness of another's distress, together with a desire to alleviate it. In short, to have compassion is to not only be aware of the needs or sufferings of others but to have a desire to aid or remedy to resolve the problem.

When we are Attentive and Compassionate to other people, it makes them feel appreciated and understood, which makes them more willing to hear what you have to say.

Compassionate communication allows us to respond more effectively to people, especially difficult people, and better manage tough situations.

> *"The purpose of human life is to serve and to show compassion and the will to help others."*
> *Albert Schweitzer*

Compassionate communication helps you to remain empathetic, even in situations filled with frustration. It enables you to take accountability, resist the urge to engage in the blame game, and gracefully accept personal criticism.

Compassionate communication produces the following skills:

- Active Listening – Carefully listen to the person's concern without interruption.

- Empathy – Be patient with the person and imagine

yourself in their place.

- Communicating with proper tone and grammar

  - ➢ Showing compassion and concern
  - ➢ Apologizing, if necessary
  - ➢ Offering an amicable solution

Compassionate Communication Techniques

Pausing – is about appreciating silence, taking the time to pause before and after saying something.

Label the feelings – this involves active listening, especially when a person is angry or frustrated. In such situations it is important to understand the emotions behind the words. Understanding is the prerequisite to problem-solving. If you do not understand the person, how can you help them to resolve an issue? When trying to understand, it is good to use common phrases like, "I hear, or I heard (whatever emotion you perceived), "You seem" or "You sound like." Do not tell people how they are feeling, only how they sound like they are feeling to you. Avoid using words that offer no solution. Instead, offer to assist as much as possible. Be respectful, speak softly, be calm, and be an attentive listener to the person's concerns.

If your perceptions are inaccurate, the person will correct you and may be grateful to know that you are actively listening.

Be attentive to recognize that an emotion may be missing and listen for conflicting emotions. This is not the technique to use when you are verbally attacked.

"I feel like" – this technique allows you to inform a person of how they are making you feel and why you may feel a certain way, and what they can do to correct the situation. This should be done in a non-threatening manner that does not make the other party defensive. This method is best for situations that involve intense emotions that are aimed at you. This helps to refocus the person and stop the verbal attacking.

Encouraging words – Using words like "Oh?" "Really?" and "When?" are great ways to let the other person know that you are listening without interfering with the flow of conversation. This also helps you to build a better rapport.

Reflecting – This involves repeating the last word or phrase spoken by the person in question form. This is effective because you are using the person's own words and asking for more input without guiding the thoughts of the person. Furthermore, it allows you to gather information to ask an important question when you lack such detail. This is a helpful technique to allow the person to think about what you said.

Open-Ended Questions – The purpose here is to get the person talking. These questions encourage the person to talk more without directing or steering the conversation. This helps you to obtain more information with fewer questions. Open-ended questions begin with how, what, when, and where. Why is not involved because that tends to cast blame, pass judgment, and stop communications. Such a question could be "what solution would you like to see that would make you happy?"

Paraphrasing – This is an effective technique to demonstrate that you are attentive, compassionate, and empathetic because it shows that you have heard and understood. You may begin effective paraphrasing by using words like, "Are you saying…" or "Are you telling me." Furthermore, paraphrasing enables you to clarify, highlight concerns, and produce positive information sharing between you and the person. Such as, "are you saying that if we would do this, you will be happy with the resolution to this issue?" Let me see what we can do. Continue to offer solutions until the matter is resolved.

Once a resolution is reached, thank them for calling and apologize for any inconvenience. If possible, follow-up by text or email.

> *"Compassion is to look beyond our own pain, to see the pain of others."*
> *Yasmin Mogah*

#2 - Humility

"Be concerned about more than your own comforts, desire to serve the needs of others. Do not act selfishly or with rebellious motives, but in all things, conduct yourself with an attitude of humility."
Renée L. Brown

Humility is defined as a modest or low view of one's importance. Humility is a key character trait because it produces honor and respect for others and from others. Humble people are not arrogant or self-interested. They are willing to listen, learn, and thankful to be of service to another.

> *"True humility is not thinking less of yourself; it is thinking of yourself less."*
> *C.S. Lewis*

Humility is vital to a healthy workplace because it is what allows individuals to build relationships whereby all parties are valued regardless of position or status. It takes humility to have cooperation because to cooperate is to respect the thoughts and abilities of others. Humbled people allow their work and efforts to speak for them.

They are not inclined to be boastful or braggadocios. Moreover, humility is necessary to adhere to rules and procedures that you may not particularly agree with. In the workplace, humility can be shown by acknowledging a person's loss (i.e., death of a loved one, loss of job), or celebrating a milestone (birth of a child, marriage, new home purchase, end of health treatment).

A group of humbled employees is more likely to collaborate

with others because there is no fear of being put down, and they are more apt to honor the rules because they care more about "us" and less about "I."

How to Demonstrate Humility

- Listen more and talk less.

- Respect the opinions of others.

- Be accountable and admit mistakes.

- Be open-minded, willing to receive new ideas, including those that contradict your own.

- Give your best without expecting recognition from others.

- Take the initiative.

- Show appreciation.

- Ask for help.

- Compliment others.

- Self-reflect – accurately assess your own strengths and weaknesses.

#3 - Attentive

"I became very attentive to customers because I was desperate not to have people leave and never come back."
– Andrew Cherng

Attentive is defined as paying close attention to something, and according to most American dictionaries to be attentive is also to be mindful, observant, considerate, and thoughtful. In short, to be attentive is to focus on the person or task at hand. Like compassion and humility, to be attentive involves showing respect by giving your job and the customers you serve the attention they deserve.

To provide the highest quality service, you must be attentive, engaged, and completely tuned in to the moment. Pay attention to details, follow-through, and avoid procrastination.

In the workplace, to be attentive may involve noticing that the building to the left of yours is on fire; or that a coworker may be having a bad day by the somber look on their face. Being attentive means to be keenly aware of your surroundings, including people, places, and things.

Attentive Listening Means:

- You block all distractions.

- Do not rely upon memory – take notes where appropriate.

- Do not interrupt others.

- Stop multitasking.

- Recap and reflect regularly.

#4 - Resilient

"The greatest glory in living lies not in never falling, but in rising every time we fall."
Nelson Mandela

Resilient is defined by the Webster dictionary as one who is "capable of withstanding shock without permanent deformation or rupture, or one who tends to recover from or adjust easily to misfortune or change." Resilience is the ability to be like a palm tree and bounce back after being pushed down. To be resilient, one must be grounded in a belief that no matter the circumstances or situation, they can face it and rise above it, positively and proactively.

In the workplace things can happen regularly to cause you emotional distress – i.e., you have a new manager who is not so nice or helpful; new rules and procedures apply to your position, and you do not agree; a customer calls with a bad attitude; you thought that you would get a promotion, but it did not happen. Negative experiences such as these may give rise to undesirable emotions, which is why you must be resilient so that you may remain focused and peaceful.

Resilient people are those who actively seek the positive answer to adverse situations.

A resilient person is one who can deal with day to day work stresses. They do not allow changes or failures to consume them; instead, they adapt, adjust, and remain committed to high performance.

How to Build and Demonstrate Resilience

- Recognize the difference between what is true and what you feel.

- Utilize support systems – i.e., family, friends, and professional counselors.

- Seek the lesson and positive purpose in everyone and everything.

- Treat challenges as an opportunity to grow.

- Accept change as natural, normal, and unavoidable.

- Manage emotions and negative thinking.

- Help the person to focus on corrective action rather than emotions. Focusing on the corrective action can help to diminish the person's emotions.

#5 - Assertive

"Once you have a major success with assertiveness, you learn that it's a much healthier path than being a doormat to the insensitive folks. You gain respect for yourself, have more time for your priorities, and develop authentic and healthier relationships." Doreen Virtue

To be assertive is to have the ability to express your thoughts and feelings appropriately, confidently, and effectively without attacking or putting down another. Assertive people understand that they not only have rights but responsibilities, and they are willing to make it known.

Assertive people are vital to the workplace because:

> 1. They are not afraid to ask for help

> 2. They will inform their superior if they do not have the tools to complete the task assigned or that they have too many conflicting priorities

> 3. They have the confidence to do their job with the highest level of excellence.

When an assertive individual is confronted with an unethical situation, they will hold firm to their values and respectfully decline.

"Assertiveness is not what you do, it's who you are!" Shakti Gawain

Assertiveness is essential to good character because one must be able to assert their rights and responsibilities. Furthermore, it is through assertiveness that compassion manifests.

Being assertive is not aggressive or arrogance, but the ability to gracefully stand your ground.

How to Develop and Demonstrate Assertiveness

- Actively listen.

- Accept that it is okay to disagree.

- Remain calm and cool.

- Be open and honest.

> *"To be passive is to let others decide for you. To be aggressive is to decide for others. To be assertive is to decide for yourself. And to trust that there is enough, that you are enough."*
> *Edith Eva Eger*

#6 - Conscientious

"Change the way you look at things and the things you look at will change."
Wayne Dyer

According to the American Psychological Association Dictionary, 2007 - Conscientious is the tendency to be organized, responsible, and hardworking. A conscientious person is said to be ambitious, committed, efficient, organized, not lazy, or impulsive. They take time to ensure accuracy and high quality.

"To accomplish great things, we must not only act, but also dream; not only plan, but also believe."
Anatole France

A conscientious person takes pride in their work. They plan and take the necessary steps to execute effectively, completing tasks with little to no errors. Furthermore, such persons tend to be more persistent, resilient, and engaged in their work, which leads to better quality performance.

A conscientious attitude adds value to you personally because it produces a skill that builds your reputation for being a person of character; one people can trust. Therefore, causing others to see you as a dependable and reliable leader.

How to develop and demonstrate Conscientiousness

Multitask less and focus more.

Increase your awareness of self and others by asking yourself questions like:

1. How conscientious are you?
2. Do you finish work before surfing the internet, or do you google throughout the day?
3. Do you plan ahead or take days as they come?
4. Do you check the detail before signing off on projects or race straight on to your next task?
5. How present in each moment are you?
6. How easy do you find it to clear your mind and concentrate on tasks?
7. Do you struggle with details and deadlines because you do not enjoy the assignment or see it as unimportant?
8. Does the work you do conflict with your beliefs?
9. Do you value building relationships with colleagues, collaboration, and teamwork?
10. Do others consider you to be conscientious and a good team member?

> *"No problem can be solved from the same level of consciousness that created it."*
> *Albert Einstein*

#7 - Thankful

What does it mean to be thankful? The dictionary say's that it means to be pleased and relieved; to express gratitude and relief. However, to grasp the full concept, we must go deeper.

A person who is thankful is one who has learned to find appreciation in everything and is grateful for all things. A thankful person does not let all that is wrong overshadow the much of what is right. A thankful person is conscious of the fact that life in and of itself is enough to be thankful for.

Thankfulness is the bedrock of the other eight C.H.A.R.A.C.T.E.R. principles and is one of the best ways to develop strong relationships.

> *"Gratitude makes sense of our past, brings peace for today, and creates vision for tomorrow."*
> Melody Beattie

Being thankful goes a long way. When you say thank you to family, friends, colleagues, and even your manager you are communicating goodness and kindness. This, in turn, creates an energy in you and others that makes for a more creative and enjoyable workplace.

Thankfulness sees potential in others, removes fear, and builds trust, creates hope, and fosters resilience.

When gratitude is expressed, everyone wins!

Ways to Develop and Demonstrate Thankfulness

Write a letter expressing thankfulness:

- Clearly state what you are grateful for. Start by saying, "thank you for ...."

- Mention how the action/behavior you are grateful for was helpful to you.

- Acknowledge the sacrifices that the person you are grateful for has made.

- Recognize the character strength exhibited by the person to whom you are saying thank you.

#8 - Enthusiastic

"Enthusiasm is one of the most powerful engines of success. When you do a thing, do it with all your might. Put your whole soul into it. Stamp it with your own personality. Be active, be energetic, and faithful, and you will accomplish your object. Nothing great was ever achieved without enthusiasm."
Ralph Waldo Emerson

To be enthusiastic means to conduct oneself with positive energy that is visible and even contagious to others. Enthusiastic people not only have a positive attitude, but they are conscientious because they take pride in their work. They are more confident and optimistic about their abilities. Furthermore, enthusiastic people are team players and high performers who add value to the organization's bottom line.

Most employers would rather have an inexperienced enthusiastic person than an unenthused, highly skilled person.

Enthusiasm in the workplace may be demonstrated in a variety of ways. For instance, smiling, making eye contact, and performing duties in a cheerful manner. Enthusiastic workers are more willing to listen, learn, and try new things.

"An enthusiastic heart finds opportunities everywhere."
Paulo Coelho

Those who provide customer service are more likely to be attentive, show compassion, and be proactive with customers. Additionally, when things are slow, the enthusiastic employee will take the initiative to seek other work opportunities.

In short, an enthusiastic employee is one who is thankful to be at work, willing to go above and beyond the call of duty; and glad to be of service to their peers and the organization at large.

How to Develop and Demonstrate Enthusiasm

Ask yourself these questions:

- What does it mean to have a positive attitude?

- What does a positive attitude look like to others?

- What does it mean to have a negative attitude?

- What does a negative attitude look like to others?

- How can you maintain a positive attitude when you are doing something that you do not like or agree with?

Then Decide to do the Following:

- Smile

- Do not be discouraged by disappointments and failures.

- Treat every assignment or project as important.

- Encourage and support others.

> *"Success consists of going from failure to failure without loss of enthusiasm."*
> *Winston Churchill*

#9 - Reliable

*"Ability is important in our quest for success, but
dependability is critical."*
Zig Ziglar

To be reliable is to be a person whom others may depend
upon and trust. A reliable person is honest. You can
believe what they tell you.

Reliability in the workplace is vital to an individual's
performance. A reliable person is one who reports to work
on time and is ready to perform his/or duties in a timely
manner. A reliable person does what they say and
communicates timely if they perform as promised.

*"Whoever is careless
with the truth in
small matters cannot
be trusted with
important matters."*
Albert Einstein

Reliable individuals are also Conscientious and
Enthusiastic. They are dependable for meeting
deadlines, being detail-oriented, supporting
colleagues, management, and
organizational objectives. Moreover, reliable people do
not require constant supervising or micro-managing.

How to Develop and Demonstrate Reliability

- Be proactive.

- Finish what you start.

- Be honest, no matter what.

- Respect your time and that of others.

- Hold firm to your values.

32

> *"I prefer to be true to myself, even at the hazard of incurring the ridicule of others, rather than to be false, and to incur my own abhorrence."*
> *Frederick Douglass*

Training in Review

Assess whether exposure to this **C.H.A.R.A.C.T.E.R.** and Soft-Skills Development Training has been effective by group participation or individual discussion about the following scenarios:

- A loyal customer is upset about a service contract with an appliance that does not work properly. (Note: The customer has a limited-service contract.) What do you do?

- A co-worker has procrastinated in completing their tasks, which renders your task completion being delayed. (Note: Your emotions are high, and the co-worker senses your frustration.) How should this situation be handled?

- Your team has been given an assignment, and you are the team leader; however, a member of your team is micro-managing the team members making it difficult to work together. As the team leader how do you resolve this, so there is a cohesive working relationship?

About Renée L. Brown

Coach, Consultant, Speaker, Teacher, and Writer

Renée holds a bachelor's degree in Business Administration, a master's degree in Public Administration, and a Juris Doctor Law degree. She has published numerous articles and one academic book. Renée will empower you to reevaluate your priorities and values. She will encourage you to have faith in yourself and the plans of the Creator. She will inspire and motivate you to risk it all to achieve your dreams and refuse to settle. But most of all she will impart the knowledge you need to ignite the fire in you for the life you desire.

BE AUTHENTICALLY FEARLESS

You are not the things you do or do not have. You are not the job you hold or a loser because you do not have one. You are not worth more or less because of your economic status, gender, race, religion, or sex.

BUT YOU ARE WHAT YOU BELIEVE!

Do you want to live authentically, face and overcome fears, become more resilient, and dare to dream again? Then you want to bring Renée in to give you an electrifying and eloquent speech that is funny, interesting, and will motivate you to do whatever it takes to discover your true character, develop the courage to be you, and live
AUTHENTICALLY FEARLESS.

What People Say About Renée L. Brown

"Renée has a powerful way of pulling the listener in to her story. She takes ideas and makes them personal and relevant while also entertaining her audience!"

Melanie Thornton, MA, CPACC University of Arkansas

"Renée is a great speaker! She can deliver a serious message with humor and sensitivity. I think this woman is going to make a difference not only here in Arkansas, but all over the world."

Jacqueline Cheek, RN, PHD, Victim Services Provider

If you are interested in Renée as a keynote speaker, motivational speaker, panelist, or workshop presenter, contact her at:

✉ Reneebrown1@yahoo.com

🖥 www.girlfriendsofvirtue.com

☎ (248) 250-0159